Language Olympics Advanced

MW00379713

Name _____

Lesson 1
- ❑ Introduction
- ❑ Vocabulary
- ❑ Story - *Gabriel's Announcements*
- ❑ Review
- ❑ Reflection
- ❑ Notes

Lesson 2
- ❑ Background History
- ❑ Vocabulary
- ❑ Story - *Birth of Messiah*
- ❑ Review
- ❑ Reflection
- ❑ Notes

Lesson 3
- ❑ Background History
- ❑ Vocabulary
- ❑ Story - *Baptism and Temptation*
- ❑ Review
- ❑ Reflection
- ❑ Notes

Lesson 4
- ❑ Background History
- ❑ Vocabulary
- ❑ Story - *Two Rulers*
- ❑ Review
- ❑ Reflection
- ❑ Notes

Lesson 5
- ❑ Background History
- ❑ Vocabulary
- ❑ Story - *Woman at the Well*
- ❑ Review
- ❑ Reflection
- ❑ Notes

Lesson 6
- ❑ Background History
- ❑ Vocabulary
- ❑ Story - *Sermon on the Mount*
- ❑ Review
- ❑ Reflection
- ❑ Notes

Lesson 7
- ❑ Background History
- ❑ Vocabulary
- ❑ Story - *Fishing for People*
- ❑ Review
- ❑ Reflection
- ❑ Notes

Lesson 8
- ❑ Background History
- ❑ Vocabulary
- ❑ Story - *Forgiving Sins*
- ❑ Review
- ❑ Reflection
- ❑ Notes

Lesson 9
- ❑ Background History
- ❑ Vocabulary
- ❑ Story - *Healing and Teaching*
- ❑ Review
- ❑ Reflection
- ❑ Notes

Lesson 10
- ❑ Background History
- ❑ Vocabulary
- ❑ Story - *Power to Change*
- ❑ Review
- ❑ Reflection
- ❑ Notes

Copyright © by John & Jan Walsh ◆ Cover Design by Joe Horine
2905 Gill Street ◆ Bloomington IL 61704 ◆ U.S.A. ◆ Version 1.01 ◆ September 2019
Email: info@ LanguageOlympics.org

Suggested Procedures

Overview

- This course is designed for advanced students who are able to read and write in English.
- One-on-one tutoring is helpful for this study.
- Your tutor is a person who sits alongside you, converses with you, and checks your work. This person will listen to you read aloud. He/she can be your discussion partner and will also give you help in using correct spelling, grammar, and sentence structure.

Supplies

- Pencils for all written activities
- Green pen for tutor signatures

Background History

- This includes helpful facts about ancient historical happenings as well as cultural information to increase understanding of the lesson material.

Quick Definitions

- We provide these short definitions in order to aid understanding of the material. These will be especially helpful for students who have not studied the 30 stories in the Language Olympics Old Testament series.

Vocabulary Words

- Each lesson has a list of vocabulary words. Knowing the meanings of the vocabulary words prepares a student for reading and understanding the content of the lesson.
- Students will benefit by writing the defnition (meaning) of each vocabulary word or phrase and using it in a sentence.
- If the student's native language is not English, the definition can be written in whichever language is most helpful.

Reading the Story Aloud

- Reading aloud is an opportunity to practice correct pronunciation of words. In addition, the reader should use expression, pauses, and rhythm that make the spoken text pleasant and easy for the listener to understand.

Lesson Review

- The student should try to fill in the blanks without looking back at the previous pages. However, he/she may look back if needed.

Telling the Story

- To demonstrate comprehension and mastery, the student tells the lesson story in simple conversational English.

Reflection and Questions

- To receive the maximum benefit from these advanced studies, it is important to spend time reflecting—thinking deeply and carefully—on the happenings and concepts presented in the lesson.

Conversation

- This course places great importance on learning to converse, using correct pronunciation and sentence structure.
- Dialogue about the ideas presented in the lessons is also an effective way to internalize the truth of Scripture.

Writing Assignments

- Learning to express thoughts in writing is an important part of mastering English language skills for everyday use.
- The "Notes" page in each lesson may be used for answering Reflection questions or any other writing activities desired.

Review Quizzes

- These exercises review names of important people and places, as well as significant quotations from various characters.

Crossword Puzzles

- The crossword puzzles reinforce important information presented in the lessons and provide a review of vocabulary words.

Map of Israel

Familiarize yourself with the places on this map,
and refer to it often as you do the lessons.

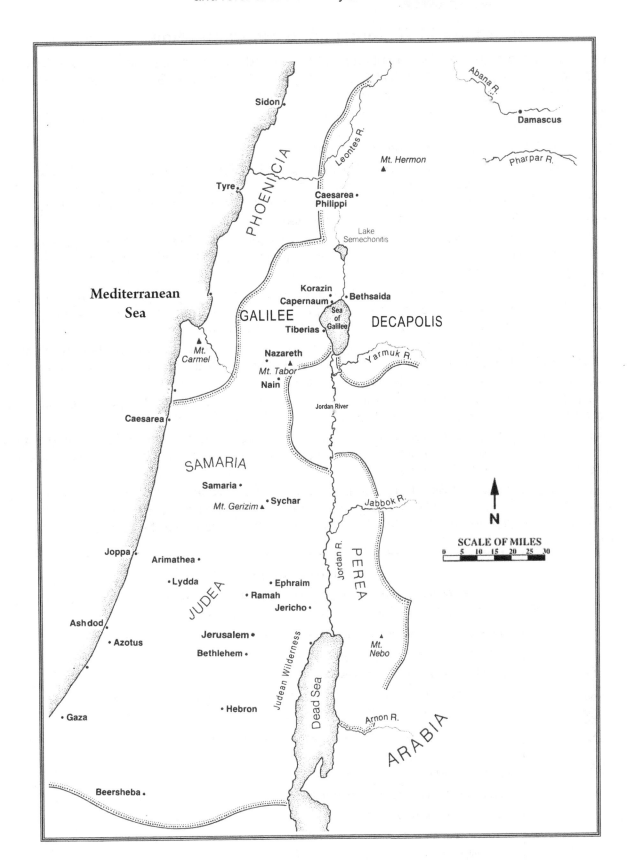

Introduction

☐ **Read this page before starting Lesson 1.**

After the Old Testament and before the New Testament

When the times of the Old Testament ended, Persia ruled the Jewish people. Around 300 BC, Alexander the Great, of Greece, defeated the Persians and established Greek language and culture throughout Israel, Egypt, Syria, and all the other countries he ruled.

When Alexander died, his kingdom was divided into four parts. At first, Israel was under the part based in Egypt. During that time, many Jews lived in the Egyptian city of Alexandria. In fact, it had the largest population of Jews in any foreign location.

In 63 B.C. the Romans came into power. They appointed Herod the Great as ruler over the Jews who lived in and around Jerusalem. Herod was known as a great builder. He completed several construction projects, including the fortress of Masada and a deep-water seaport at Caesarea. Herod pleased the Jews by re-building and expanding the Temple at Jerusalem.

King Herod, however, was also known for being extremely cruel. He always feared that someone would kill him in order to become king in his place. He had many of his own family members killed, including his wife and three of his sons.

At this point in history, there had been about 400 years of "silence" from God—years that no prophets were bringing messages from God. The Jewish people were living under the rule of foreign powers. Still, they believed that their Messiah would come to deliver them.

The Hebrew word *messiah* means 'anointed one'. The Jewish people expected their messiah to be a 'savior' who would deliver them from Roman rule and make Israel an independent nation once again. *Messiah* is translated *Christ* in the Greek language. *(John 1:41)*

The prophet Isaiah foretold that the Anointed One would come to deliver the people of Israel. He also said that another person would come to prepare the way of the Lord. *(Isaiah 61:1 & 40:3)*

The Jewish people were descendants of Abraham, a person who was known for obeying God. They proudly called him "our father, Abraham." God promised Abraham that his descendants would be a blessing to all the world. *(Genesis 22:18)*

The entire Old Testament Scriptures had been preparing people for the coming of Messiah. They foretold that his mother would be a young virgin, that he would be born in Bethlehem, and that he would bring salvation to the whole world. The *New Testament* tells about the birth, life, and work of Jesus.

Quick Definitions

God: the perfect all-powerful being who created and rules the world

angel: a spiritual being that serves as a messenger from God

anoint: to put oil on someone; to officially choose someone for a special task

foretell: to tell something before it happens; to prophesy

Gentile: a person who is not Jewish

priest: a person who has the authority to perform ceremonies in a religious service

prophet: a person who delivers messages from God

prophecy: a statement that something will happen in the future

religion: belief in God; worship of God

Rabbi: a teacher in the Jewish religion

salvation: the act of saving someone from sin or evil

savior: someone who saves a person

Scriptures: holy writings of God's prophets; a holy book

sin: evil; something done against God's law

virgin: a person who has not had sexual intercourse

Vocabulary 1

☐ Write the meanings of these words.
☐ Write a sentence of your own, using each word or a form of that word.

to appear _____

_____

culture _____

_____

to defeat _____

_____

to deliver _____

_____

descendant _____

_____

to describe _____

_____

to exclaim _____

_____

foreign _____

_____

to be forgiven _____

_____

to fulfill _____

_____

to imagine _____

_____

perspective _____

_____

to praise _____

_____

to reply (replied) _____

_____

worthy _____

_____

☐ My student knows the meaning of these words.   Tutor initials _____

☐ My student has used the word correctly in a sentence.   Tutor initials _____

5

Lesson 1 ◈ Gabriel's Announcements

Scriptures: Luke 1:5-45, 56-79

Zechariah and Elizabeth were people who obeyed the Lord. They did not have any children and, in time, they were past the childbearing years.

Zechariah was a priest who served God faithfully. One day, he was in the Temple in Jerusalem, giving an offering to the Lord. People gathered and waited outside, praying.

Suddenly, an angel appeared to Zechariah! The angel said, "Don't be afraid! God has heard your prayers. Your wife, Elizabeth will have a son, and you must name him John. He will have the same power as the prophet Elijah had. He will bring you joy, and he will be a great servant of the Lord. God's spirit will be on him from the time he is born. He will help many people turn back to God, and he will prepare the way for Messiah."

Zechariah asked, "How can I know this will really happen? My wife and I are too old."

The angel answered, "My name is Gabriel, and I was sent to give you this good news. You have not believed me. Therefore, you will not be able to speak until everything I have told you happens."

After the angel left, Zechariah went outside where the people were waiting. He tried to say something, but he couldn't talk. So the people knew he had seen a vision.

The priest went home, and soon, Elizabeth was expecting a child.

Six months later, that same angel, Gabriel, went to the town of Nazareth and appeared to a young woman named Mary. She was engaged to marry a man named Joseph. Both of them were descendants of King David.

The angel said, "Mary, you are blessed by God. Don't be afraid. God is pleased with you. You will give birth to a son and call his name Jesus. He will be great, and there will be no end to his kingdom."

Mary looked at the angel and asked, "How can this be true? I am a virgin."

"The Holy Spirit will come upon you, and the power of God will cause this to happen. Your child will be called the Son of God. Nothing is impossible with God! Even your cousin Elizabeth is expecting a baby in her old age."

Mary replied, "I am the servant of the Lord. May this happen just as you have said."

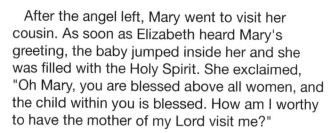

After the angel left, Mary went to visit her cousin. As soon as Elizabeth heard Mary's greeting, the baby jumped inside her and she was filled with the Holy Spirit. She exclaimed, "Oh Mary, you are blessed above all women, and the child within you is blessed. How am I worthy to have the mother of my Lord visit me?"

Mary stayed with this wise older woman for three months. Then she went back home to her family.

After Mary left, Elizabeth gave birth to her baby boy. Neighbors and family members came to rejoice with the old couple. They said, "Your son should be called Zechariah."

Elizabeth said, "No, his name is John."

"John? There's no one in your family named John. We'll talk to Zechariah about this."

The priest wrote on a tablet, *His name is John.* Immediately, he was filled with God's spirit and began speaking. "Praise the Lord God of Israel! He is fulfilling the promise he made to our father, Abraham.

He picked up his son. "You, my child, will be a prophet of God to prepare the way for Messiah. You will tell people how they can be saved by having their sins forgiven.

The Promised One—our Messiah—will bring light to those who sit in darkness and the fear of death. He will guide us into the way of peace.

☐ **My student has read the story aloud.** Tutor initials _____

Lesson 1 Review

☐ Fill in the blanks with the best answer.

1. Abraham was known for _____ God.

2. God promised Abraham that his _____ would be a blessing to all the world.

3. The Hebrew word *messiah* means '*anointed one*'. It is translated _____ in Greek.

4. The prophet Isaiah foretold that the Anointed One would come to _____ the people of

   Israel. He also said that another person would come to _____ the way of the Lord.

5. Zechariah and _____ were people who obeyed the Lord. They didn't have any children.

6. An _____ appeared to Zechariah in the Temple and told him that he and his wife would have

   a son. They were to name him _____ , and he would prepare the way for _____.

7. When Zechariah didn't _____ the message, the angel said, "You will not be able to

   _____ until everything I have told you happens."

8. Six months later, that same angel, Gabriel, went to the town of Nazareth and appeared to a

   young woman named _____. She was engaged to marry a man named _____.

9. The angel told Mary, "You will give birth to a son and call his name _____."

10. Mary asked, "How can this be true? I am a _____."

11. The angel answered, "The Holy _____ will come upon you, and the _____ of God

    will cause this to happen. Your child will be called the _____ of _____."

12. After the angel left, Mary went to visit her _____, Elizabeth.

13. Elizabeth exclaimed, "How am I _____ to have the mother of my _____ visit me!"

14. Mary stayed with this wise older woman for _____ months, and then she went back home.

15. When Elizabeth gave birth to her baby boy, neighbors and family members said, "Your son should

    be called _____." The priest wrote on a tablet ...*His name is* _____.

16. Immediately, Zechariah was filled with God's spirit and began speaking. "Praise the Lord God of

    Israel! He is _____ the promise he made to our father, Abraham."

17. He picked up his son. "You, my child, will be a prophet of God to _____ the way for

    Messiah. You will tell people how they can be saved by having their sins _____.

    The Promised One—our _____—will bring light to those who sit in darkness and the

    fear of _____. He will guide us into the way of peace."

☐ Checked by Tutor   Tutor initials _____

☐ My student has told the story aloud in his/her own words.   Tutor initials _____   7

Reflection and Questions
Lesson 1 ◈ Gabriel's Announcements

❏ Read the questions on this page.

❏ Tell your thoughts aloud and/or write your answers on the next page.

Your perspective:

- Tell about someone you know who "obeys the Lord."

- Tell about someone you know who had their prayers answered.

Review the facts:

- Where was Zechariah when he had a vision? What was he doing?

- The angel, Gabriel, gave a message to two people. Who were they?

Search for answers:

- What happened that made Zechariah believe what the angel said?

- What helped Mary believe the message the angel gave her?

Writing assignments:

- Look up the prophecies in *Isaiah 7:14* and *Micah 5:2*.
  Copy them on the next page.

- Imagine you are Mary:
    (1) Write a few sentences about what you were thinking as you were traveling to
       the home of Elizabeth and Zechariah.
    (2) Write a few sentences about what you were thinking as you traveled home
       after visiting with Elizabeth and Zechariah.

Final thoughts:

- What was your favorite part of the story? Why?

Notes

☐ My student's English grammar and sentence structure is correct. Tutor initials ________

Background History for Lesson 2

The Roman Empire

During the time of Christ, the Roman Empire included all the lands around the Mediterranean Sea, and most of Northwest Europe. God used the Romans to bring about several important changes before the coming of the Messiah. These included a common language, an excellent road system, the rule of law, and peace.

Caesar Augustus became emperor in 27 B.C. and ruled until 14 A.D. One set of laws governed the whole empire, and officers were hired to carry out the Emperor's policies. One of these men was King Herod.

Caesar Augustus ordered a "taxation" about every 10 years during his reign. The word *tax* meant *register*. Every man had to go and register in the home town of his ancestors. A census was taken in order to have an official listing of citizens. It was for the purpose of collecting taxes, and also for the emperor to know how many people were in his kingdom.

Bethlehem

Bethlehem was about five miles south of Jerusalem. David was born in Bethlehem, and he was anointed king there. Joseph was a descendant of King David, so Joseph and Mary had to go to Bethlehem to register for the census.

In the hills of Bethlehem, a house often had a room where there was a living area for the family, and another place, near the door, where their animals were kept at night. This provided safety for the animals. Also, their body heat could help warm the home on cool nights. The area for the animals would have had a manger (feeding trough). It is probable that Joseph and Mary stayed in a room such as this on the night Jesus was born.

The Wise Men

Hundreds of years before Christ, Jews were taken to Persia. At the time of Christ's birth, many Jews still lived there, and they knew the teachings about a coming Messiah. The "wise men" may have come from Persia, since they were called *magi*, which is from a Persian word meaning *religious scholars*. According to Eastern customs, offerings were given as a way of showing honor to kings. Gifts of gold, frankincense, and myrrh were worth a lot of money. These gifts that they brought may have helped Joseph pay for his family's journey to Egypt.

Nazareth

Nazareth is about 88 miles north of Jerusalem, halfway between the Mediterranean Sea and the Sea of Galilee. Nazareth was an agricultural village of several hundred people, most of whom made their living growing grapes, olives, corn and flax. As a young man, Jesus probably helped in the seasonal harvesting of those crops.

Joseph worked in Nazareth as a carpenter. At that time a carpenter was a craftsman, who worked in construction, both with stone and wood.

Education

Education was important to Jewish families. Children memorized verses of Scripture and wise sayings. Girls were taught homemaking skills by their mothers, and boys were taught to read by their fathers. A boy's father would also teach him a job skill. Boys began studying Jewish law at age ten. They would learn together from a Rabbi at their local synagogue. Eventually, a young man could go to a highly respected teacher and become a *disciple*, often following him from place to place in order to learn through daily discussions and activities.

Quick Definitions

census: official count of the total number of people in a country

decree: official order given by a government or a person with power

disciple: follower of a famous person; one who helps to spread the teachings of that person

glory: public praise and honor

magi: official way to refer to the "wise men" who came to worship the young child, Jesus

memorable: something worth remembering

taught: past tense of *'teach'*

Vocabulary 2

☐ Write the meanings of these words.
☐ Write a sentence of your own, using each word or a form of that word.

activity/activities _____

ancestors _____

available _____

to collect _____

to discuss _____

engagement _____

to flee (fled) _____

guest room _____

intimate _____

manger _____

register _____

religious _____

to require _____

to shame _____

to warn _____

☐ My student knows the meaning of these words.   Tutor initials _____

☐ My student has used the word correctly in a sentence.   Tutor initials _____

11

Lesson 2 ◈ Birth of the Messiah

Matthew 1:18-25; Matthew 2:1-23; Luke 2:1-20; Luke 2:40, 51-52

When Mary arrived home, Joseph found out she was expecting a child. He knew he was not the father, but he loved Mary and didn't want to shame her. He decided to simply break off their engagement.

As he was deep in thought about this, an angel appeared to him in a dream. "Joseph, don't be afraid to take Mary as your wife. The child within her is from the Holy Spirit. When the baby is born, name him Jesus. He is the promised one who will save his people from their sins."

Joseph did not hesitate. He took Mary as his wife. But, he was not intimate with her until after the child was born.

Joseph and Mary lived in Nazareth, in the northern part of Israel. Yet, the Old Testament prophets had written in the Scriptures that Messiah would be born in Bethlehem, in the south near Jerusalem. Then Caesar decided to tax his entire empire. His order required all people to register in the town of their ancestors. Joseph's family was from Bethlehem, so he and Mary had to go there.

Some days after they arrived, the time came for Mary's baby to be born. There were no guest rooms available, so they stayed in a sleeping area next to where animals were kept at night. When the baby was born, he was wrapped in strips of cloth and laid in a manger.

That night, shepherds were watching their sheep in a field nearby. Suddenly an angel appeared, and the place was filled with a bright light. The shepherds were terrified! The angel spoke, "Don't be afraid. I'm here to bring you good news! Tonight, the Savior has been born in Bethlehem. He is Messiah, Christ the Lord. Go there, and look for a baby wrapped in strips of cloth, lying in a manger." Then more angels appeared, saying, "Glory to God in the highest! Peace and good will to the earth."

The shepherds did as they were told. They hurried to Bethlehem and found Mary, Joseph, and the baby, just as the angel had said. The shepherds told everyone about the Christ child. Then they went back to their fields, praising God for what they had seen.

Sometime after the birth of Jesus, wise men came from the east. Their studies showed that a new king would one day come to Israel. They studied the stars and were sure that this king had finally been born. So they went to Jerusalem and talked to King Herod who ruled over Israel. They asked, "Where is the child who has been born to be King of the Jews? We have seen his star, and have come to worship him."

Herod was evil and cruel. Anger rose within him when he heard about a new king being born in his kingdom. But he controlled himself and told the men he would look into the matter. He called for the priests and religious teachers to come before him. "Where does the Scripture say Messiah is to be born?"

They were quick to answer. "Oh, he is to be born in Bethlehem, just as the prophets wrote."

Herod told that to his visitors. He said, "Go find the child. Then come back and let me know. I want to go worship him, too."

The men looked up and saw the same star they had seen in the east. It moved ahead of them, to Bethlehem, and then it stopped right over the house where Joseph, Mary, and the young child lived. The *magi* bowed down before Jesus and worshiped him. They gave him gifts of gold, frankincense, and myrrh. Then they were warned in a dream not to return to King Herod, so they went home a different way.

That night, an angel appeared to Joseph. "Get up! Take your family to Egypt, and stay there until I tell you to return. Herod is sending soldiers to kill the child." So Joseph got up in the night and fled with his family to Egypt.

When Herod realized that the wise men had not obeyed him, he was extremely angry! He ordered soldiers to go to Bethlehem and kill all the young boys two years of age and younger.

After several years in Egypt, Joseph was visited by an angel of the Lord who told him that Herod had died, and it was safe to return to Israel. So, Joseph moved his family to Nazareth. There, Jesus spent his early years with his parents. He grew, became strong, and was filled with wisdom. He was respected by all who knew him, and God's blessing was on his life.

☐ My student has read the story aloud.   Tutor initials _____

Lesson 2 Review

Fill in the blanks with the best answer.

1. When Mary arrived home, Joseph found out she was _____.

2. He knew he was not the father, but he loved Mary and didn't want to _____ her. Therefore, he decided to simply break off their _____.

3. An _____ appeared to Joseph and told him he should take Mary as his wife. The angel said, . . . "The child within her is from the _____ _____. When the baby is born, name him _____. He is the _____ one who will save his people from their sins.

4. Joseph and Mary lived in _____, in the northern part of Israel.

5. Caesar's order _____ all people to register in the town of their _____. Joseph's family was from _____, so he and Mary had to go there.

6. When Mary's baby was born, he was wrapped in strips of cloth and laid in a _____.

7. That night, an angel appeared to _____ who were watching their sheep nearby.

8. The angel said, "I'm here to bring you good news! Tonight, the _____ has been born in Bethlehem. He is Messiah, _____ the Lord." More angels appeared, saying, "_____ to God in the highest! _____ and good will to the earth."

9. Wise men from the east were _____ that the promised King had finally been born.

10. King Herod said, "Go find the child and come back to me. I want to go _____ him, too."

11. When the wise men found Joseph, Mary, and the young child, they _____ down before Jesus and worshiped him. They gave him _____ of gold, frankincense, and myrrh.

12. Then they were _____ in a dream not to return to King Herod, so they went home a different way.

13. That night, an angel told Joseph, "Get up! Take your family to _____, and stay there until I tell you to return. Herod is sending soldiers to _____ the child." So Joseph got up in the night and _____ with his family to Egypt.

14. When Herod realized the wise men had not obeyed him, he was _____ angry! He ordered soldiers to go to Bethlehem and kill all the young boys two years of age and younger.

15. After several years in Egypt, an angel from the Lord told Joseph that Herod had died and it was safe to return to Israel. So, Joseph moved his family to _____.

☐ Checked by Tutor   Tutor initials _____

☐ My student has told the story aloud in his/her own words.   Tutor initials _____   13

Reflection and Questions
Lesson 2 ◈ Birth of the Messiah

❑ Read the questions on this page.
❑ Tell your thoughts aloud or write your answers on the next page.

Your perspective:

- Tell about a trip you will never forget.

Review the facts:

- This story talks about various people going to Bethlehem. List four different groups of them. Which ones received a message from God?

Search for answers:

- What helped Joseph decide to take Mary as his wife?

- What helped the shepherds believe they had truly found the Messiah?

- What helped the wise men be so sure they had found the new king?

- Why did the wise men go home a different way and not report back to King Herod?

Writing assignments:

- Imagine you are Mary or Joseph, and write down your thoughts soon after the birth of Jesus.

Final thoughts:

- What difficulties do you think Joseph may have had as the earthly "father" of Jesus?

Notes

My student's English grammar and sentence structure is correct.   Tutor initials _____

Background History for Lesson 3

Clothing of John the Baptist

John the Baptist had clothes made of camel's hair, and he wore a leather belt. This was typical clothing for a country shepherd or farmer. Camel's hair is long, and easily pulled from the skin of the camel in the spring of the year. It is then woven into cloth to make clothing. Camel's hair clothing is lightweight, and it provides excellent protection from the winter's cold and summer's heat.

Food of John the Baptist

John's food was locusts and wild honey. It may not have been his only food but was something he ate for many of his meals.

Bee's honey was found in the hollows of trees and rocks. The juices of certain fruits were also called *honey*.

Locusts are rich in protein and good for food. They have long been a common food in the Middle East. Today, people in several areas of the world collect locusts for food. They are usually boiled, stir-fried, or roasted, and they are sometimes called *desert shrimps*.

Sons of Abraham

At the time of John the Baptist, Jewish people thought that a person's salvation was based on being a "son of Abraham"—being part of a Jewish family. However, John taught that if you want to be a child of God, you need to be a true "son of Abraham"—someone who believes and obeys God like Abraham did.

Baptism

The Jewish custom of baptism was traditionally for Gentiles (non-Jews) who wanted to accept the Jewish faith. John's baptism was different.

John taught that people should prepare themselves for the coming Messiah by admitting their sins and repenting—turning away from sin. Those baptized by John admitted their sin and their need to repent.

Jesus came to John for baptism, but not for the purpose of showing repentance. Rather, he was fulfilling the Jewish custom for a priest to be anointed at 30 years of age before beginning his ministry.

In Jewish baptism, the "baptizer" stood nearby and watched. The person being baptized walked out into the water, declared his faith in God, and then crouched down under the water. Once he was completely covered, he would come up out of the water, stand up straight, and speak words of praise to God. After Jesus was baptized, he came up out of the water, and a voice from heaven spoke words of praise about him.

Judean Wilderness

The Judean wilderness is on the western shore of the Dead Sea, from Jericho southwards. Very little rain falls in this rocky area, so it is mostly dry with only a few plants. During winter it has a light covering of grass and is used as pasture land for sheep and goats. Some parts of the wilderness are inhabited. That was the area where John the Baptist lived and preached.

Quick Definitions

heaven: place where God lives

ministry: the work of a religious leader

sin: action that is wrong, against the law of God

sermon: speech about a moral or religious subject

preach: to make a speech with the goal of getting a person to believe or change their behavior

Vocabulary 3

☐ **Write the meanings of these words.**

☐ **Write a sentence of your own, using each word or a form of that word.**

to admit _____

_____

to crouch _____

_____

to declare _____

_____

to depend _____

_____

especially _____

_____

faith _____

_____

to grip _____

_____

to influence _____

_____

to insist _____

_____

to repent _____

_____

straight _____

_____

to tempt _____

_____

temptation _____

_____

tradition _____

_____

typical _____

_____

☐ **My student knows the meaning of these words.   Tutor initials** _____

☐ **My student has used the word correctly in a sentence.   Tutor initials** _____

Lesson 3 ◈ Baptism and Temptation

Scriptures: Matt 3:1-17; Matt 4:1-11; Mark 1:9-13; Luke 3:3-16; Luke 4:1-13; John 1:19-34

John the Baptist

When Zechariah and Elizabeth's son, John, became a man, he went and lived in the wilderness. There he wore clothes made of camel's hair. He ate locusts and wild honey. God's Spirit gave him great power. John preached that people should repent from their sins and turn back to God. He told them, "Don't depend on being children of Abraham. God can make children of Abraham from these stones."

John baptized those who repented of their sins and wanted to live for God. It seemed that everyone knew about John and his way of life. He became known as John the Baptist. One day, some of the religious leaders asked him, "Are you the Messiah?"

He said, "No, I am not the Christ. I am the one who was sent to prepare the way for him. He will come after me, and I am not even worthy to untie his shoes."

The Baptism of Jesus

The next day, John was baptizing at the Jordan River, when he saw Jesus coming toward him. John shouted to the crowd, "Look! Here comes the Lamb of God, who takes away the sins of the world. This is the Son of God."

Jesus walked into the water and asked John to baptize him. John was shocked and said, "No! I'm the one who should be baptized by you!"

Jesus said, "Allow this to be. It is God's will."

So John baptized Jesus in front of all the people. When Jesus came up out of the water, the sky opened, and the Spirit of God—like a dove—came down on him. Then a voice from heaven spoke, "You are my Son. I am pleased with you!"

The Temptation of Jesus

After the baptism, the Spirit of God led Jesus into the wilderness to be tempted by the devil. While he was there, he did not eat any food for forty days and forty nights. After that, hunger gripped his entire body.

Suddenly, the tempter was by his side, saying, "If you really are the Son of God, make these stones become bread so you can have something to eat."

Jesus answered, "The Scripture says, 'A person cannot live by bread alone, but by every word that comes out of God's mouth.' "

The devil took him to Jerusalem—onto the highest point of the Temple wall, where they could look down on the rocks far below.

The devil said to Jesus, "If you are the Son of God, throw yourself down off this wall. God's Word says there are angels taking care of you. They will keep you from hitting those rocks below. You won't even hurt your feet on them."

Jesus replied, "The Scripture also says that you are not to tempt God and put him to the test!"

The devil then took Jesus to a very high mountain. He made all the kingdoms of the earth appear before them. He turned to Jesus and said, "I will give you everything you see. All you have to do is bow down and worship me."

Jesus ordered him, "Leave me, Satan! The Scripture says to worship only God, and serve only God."

After that, the Devil left him. Soon, angels came to Jesus and cared for his needs.

▢ **My student has read the story aloud.**   **Tutor initials** _____

Lesson 3 Review

☐ **Fill in the blanks with the best answer.**

1. John the Baptist preached that people should prepare themselves for the coming Messiah by admitting their sins and _____—turning away from sin.

2. John told the people, "Don't _____ on being children of Abraham. God can make children of Abraham from these stones."

3. John said, "I am not the Christ. I am the one who was sent to prepare the way for him. He will come after me, and I am not even _____ to untie his shoes."

4. John was baptizing at the Jordan River, when he saw _____ coming toward him.

5. John shouted to the crowd, "Look! Here comes the Lamb of God, who takes away the _____ of the world. This is the Son of God."

6. Jesus walked into the water and asked John to _____ him. John was shocked and said, "No! I'm the one who should be baptized by you!"

7. Jesus said, "Allow this to be. It is _____ _____."

8. When Jesus came up out of the water, the sky opened, and the Spirit of God—like a dove—came down on him. Then a voice from _____ spoke, "You are my Son. I am pleased with you!"

9. The Spirit of God led Jesus into the _____ to be tempted by the devil.

10. The devil said, "If you really are the _____ of _____, make these stones become bread."

11. Jesus answered, "The Scripture says, 'A person cannot live by _____ alone, but by every _____ that comes out of God's mouth.' "

12. The devil said to Jesus, "If you are the Son of God, _____ yourself down off this wall. God's Word says there are angels taking care of you."

13. Jesus answered, "The Scripture says, "You are not to _____ God and put him to the test!"

14. The devil took Jesus to a very high mountain and made all the _____ of the earth appear before them.

15. He said to Jesus, "I will give you everything you see. All you have to do is _____ _____ and worship me."

16. Jesus ordered, "Leave me, Satan! The Scripture says to _____ only God and _____ only God."

☐ **Checked by Tutor**   **Tutor initials** _____

☐ **My student has told the story aloud in his/her own words.**   **Tutor initials** _____   19

Reflection and Questions
Lesson 3 ◈ Baptism and Temptation

☐ Read the questions on this page.
☐ Tell your thoughts aloud or write your answers on the next page.

Your perspective:

- What are your favorite foods?

- Tell about a time when you were so hungry you felt you could eat almost anything.

- Name a person you know who was able to have great influence over others.

- Why was that person respected by others?

Visualization: (optional)

- Draw a picture to show how you visualize John the Baptist.

Review the facts:

- Why did the religious leaders refuse to be baptized by John?

- During the Temptation, what were the three things Satan told Jesus to do?

Writing assignments:

- Jesus used three Old Testament Scriptures when he replied to Satan. Find these and copy them on the next page: *Deuteronomy 8:3b, Deuteronomy 6:16, Deuteronomy 6:13*

Search for answers:

- When John the Baptist said, "Don't depend on being children of Abraham," what did he mean?

- Tell some ways that the baptism of Jesus was different from others who were baptized by John.

Final thoughts:

- It was the will of God for Jesus to be baptized. Tell some more reasons Jesus may have had for asking to being baptized.

- What are some temptations people have today that are similar to the ways Jesus was tempted by Satan?

- How can the Scriptures help people resist temptations?

Notes

My student's English grammar and sentence structure is correct.   Tutor initials _____

21

Background History for Lesson 4

Synagogues

While the Jews were captives in foreign nations, they couldn't go and worship at the Temple in Jerusalem. However, they still met together to pray and listen to the reading of the Scriptures. The places where they held their meetings were called *synagogues*.

The people kept this tradition even after they came back to live in Israel. Almost every community had its own synagogue. It became the center of Jewish culture, and Jews met there every Sabbath. The rulers of the synagogue were authorities in the community.

It was traditional to begin the weekly meeting with opening prayer, then a reading from the *Law* and a reading from the *Prophets*. Next would be a sermon, sometimes from a guest rabbi or teacher. Jesus had become well known, so he was expected to teach in the synagogue whenever he visited a town.

Pharisees

Pharisees were religious leaders among the Jews. They were very careful about keeping the laws of God, as written in the Scriptures. In addition, they included their own ideas and traditions, which they felt were just as important as God's laws.

The rulers of the synagogues were usually Pharisees. They controlled the Jewish priests and supervised the education of young men.

The Pharisees always tried to keep themselves pure and holy. They worked very hard to be *righteous*—that is, to do right. Many became proud of themselves and felt they were better than other people. That attitude is known as being *self-righteous*. Even so, Jesus spent time explaining spiritual concepts to them. He genuinely wanted them to know and understand the truth.

Review - Draw lines to match the people with the correct statements about them.

Zechariah

Elizabeth

Gabriel

Isaiah

Joseph

Mary

Caesar Augustus

John the Baptist

shepherds

magi

Herod

- a righteous man who was a descendant of King David
- He was sent by God to bring messages to several people.
- She gave birth to a child when she was old.
- She was visited by an angel.
- a priest who served God faithfully
- He foretold that a virgin would give birth to a son.
- visited by heavenly beings at night in a field
- ordered everyone to be taxed (registered)
- wise men
- He was known for being cruel to everyone, including his family
- He preached that people should prepare for the coming of Messiah by repenting of their sins.

☐ Checked by Tutor   Tutor initials _____

Vocabulary 4

☐ Write the meanings of these words.
☐ Write a sentence of your own, using each word or a form of that word.

community _____

_____

compassion _____

_____

to complain _____

_____

concept _____

_____

to condemn _____

_____

eternal _____

_____

genuine _____

_____

miracle _____

_____

physical _____

_____

to plead _____

_____

to recover _____

_____

to remind _____

_____

similar _____

_____

spiritual _____

_____

truth _____

_____

☐ My student knows the meaning of these words.   Tutor initials _____

☐ My student has used the word correctly in a sentence.   Tutor initials _____

Lesson 4 ◆ Two Rulers

Scriptures: John 2:23-25; John 3:1-21; Numbers 21:4-9; John 4:46-53

A Ruler of the Jews

Jesus went to Jerusalem to celebrate the Passover. While he was there, he taught many people. They believed in him when they saw his miracles.

Nicodemus was a Pharisee and a member of the Jewish ruling council. He came to Jesus at night and said, "Teacher, we know you are from God because we see your miracles."

Jesus said, "Listen to me carefully. Unless a person is born again, he cannot see the kingdom of God."

Nicodemus asked, "How can a man get back into his mother's womb and be born a second time?"

Jesus explained, "A person needs to experience physical birth and spiritual birth. Humans give physical life to their children. But only God's spirit can give you spiritual life—a new birth—and make you a child of God.

You shouldn't be surprised. There are many things you can't see with your eyes. For example, you hear and feel the wind, but you can't see it. So it is with the Spirit of God."

Nicodemus asked, "How can these things be?"

Jesus replied, "You are a respected teacher in Israel, and you don't understand these things?" Then he reminded Nicodemus of an event that took place when the Israelites were traveling through the wilderness with Moses as their leader.

Jesus said, "The people complained against God, so he sent snakes among them, and many died. Then God told Moses to make a bronze snake and put it on a pole. Those who looked at it were healed. Others died because they refused to look. Just as Moses lifted up the bronze image of a snake on a pole, even so, I also must be lifted up, so that anyone who believes in me will have eternal life.

God loved the world so much that he sent his Son to save the world and bring eternal life to those who believe. God did not send his Son into the world to condemn its people. He sent him to save them!

Those who believe in God's Son will not be condemned. But everyone who doesn't believe in him has already been condemned for not having faith in the Son of God."

A Ruler from Capernaum

On a certain day, a highly respected ruler from Capernaum traveled to Cana, where Jesus was teaching. He spoke with Jesus, "My son is sick, and he's going to die. Please come to Capernaum and heal him."

Jesus said to him, "You're like everyone else. You won't believe unless you see miracles."

The man pleaded, "Sir, please come and heal my son! He will die if you don't come quickly."

Jesus had compassion on him and said, "Go in peace; your son will live."

The ruler suddenly believed what Jesus had told him. He turned and started walking toward home. When he was almost there, his servants met him and said, "Your son is alive!"

The man asked them about what time his son started to recover. They said, "The fever left him yesterday at one o'clock in the afternoon."

The father realized that it was at that very hour when Jesus had told him, "Your son will live." So, the ruler and his entire household believed that Jesus was the Messiah.

Jewish Daytime Hours

Jewish daytime hours began at six in the morning. According to their keeping of time, the "seventh hour" would have meant the seventh hour after that. So, one o'clock in the afternoon is the time when the ruler's son in Capernaum was healed.

☐ My student has read the story aloud.   Tutor initials _____

Lesson 4 Review

☐ **Fill in the blanks with the best answer.**

1. Pharisees were religious leaders among the Jews. They were very _____ about keeping the laws of God as written in the Scriptures. In addition, they added their own ideas and _____ which they felt were just as important as God's laws.

2. The rulers of the _____ were usually Pharisees. These men always tried to keep themselves _____ and _____. Many became _____ of themselves and felt they were _____ than other people. That is known as being *self-righteous.*

3. Even so, Jesus spent time explaining spiritual concepts to them. He _____ wanted them to know and understand the _____.

4. Jesus went to Jerusalem to celebrate the Passover. While he was there, he taught many people. They believed in him when they saw his _____.

5. Nicodemus came to Jesus at _____ and said, "Teacher, we know you are from _____ , because we see your miracles."

6. Jesus said, "Unless a person is _____ _____, he cannot see the kingdom of God."

7. Nicodemus asked, "How can a person be born a _____ time?"

8. Jesus explained, "A person needs to experience _____ birth and _____ birth. _____ give physical life to their children. But only _____ spirit can give you spiritual life—a new birth—and make you a _____ of God.

9. Jesus reminded Nicodemus, "As Moses lifted up the bronze snake on a pole, . . . Even _____, I must be lifted up, so that anyone who believes in me will have _____ life.

10. God _____ the world so much that he sent his Son to save the world and bring eternal life to those who believe. God did not send his Son into the world to _____ its people. He sent him to _____ them!"

11. A highly respected ruler from _____ traveled to where Jesus was teaching. He said, "My son is _____ and is going to die. Please come to Capernaum and _____ him."

12. Jesus said to him, "You're like everyone else. You won't believe unless you see _____."

13. The man _____, "Sir, please come and heal my son! He will die if you don't come quickly."

14. Jesus had _____ on him and said, "Go in peace; your son will live."

15. The ruler from Capernaum suddenly _____ what Jesus had told him. He turned and started heading home. When he was almost there, his servants met him and exclaimed, "_____!"

16. His son had started to _____ at the very hour when Jesus told him, "Your son will live."

17. So, the ruler and his entire _____ believed that Jesus was the _____.

☐ **Checked by Tutor**   Tutor initials _____

☐ **My student has told the story aloud in his/her own words.**   Tutor initials _____   25

Reflection and Questions
Lesson 4 ◆ Two Rulers

❑ Read the questions on this page.
❑ Tell your thoughts aloud or write your answers on the next page.

Your perspective:

- Tell about a time when you were confused about what someone was saying - until they used an example to explain what they meant.

Review the facts:

- What time of day did Nicodemus meet with Jesus?
- Why did God send Jesus into the world?

Search for answers:

- Read Numbers 21:4-9 about an event the Israelites experienced in the wilderness. Explain how that story is similar to what was happening at the time of Jesus.
- Tell how physical birth and spiritual birth are similar.

Writing assignments:

- Write a conversation the ruler from Capernaum might have had with his son who was healed.
- Imagine you are the ruler from Capernaum. Write how you would praise God for the healing of your son.

Final thoughts:

- What do you think caused the ruler from Capernaum to believe Jesus when he said, "Your son will live." ?
- Why do you think Nicodemus went to visit with Jesus at night?
- How can people know if they have experienced spiritual birth?
- What does it mean to "believe in Jesus"?
- How would you define "eternal life"?

Notes

Background History for Lesson 5

Samaritans

Samaria was a district in Israel located between Galilee in the north and Judea in the south. Samaritan history began when the Assyrian army conquered that part of Israel more than 700 years BC.

The Assyrians followed their usual policy of moving most Israelites off from their homeland, and leaving behind only the very poor. Then they brought in people from other areas—people who worshiped idols (false gods).

The remaining Israelites and the foreigners soon started marrying each other. The Jews around Jerusalem thought of the descendants of those people as a separate race, and they had great contempt for them. They were called Samaritans after Samaria, their capital city.

It was illegal for Jews and Samaritans to marry each other, and Samaritans were not allowed to offer sacrifices at the Jerusalem temple. Eventually, the Samaritans built a temple for themselves on Mount Gerizim.

> **sacrifices:** animals or birds that were killed and offered to God in order for a person to receive forgiveness of sins.

Despite their conflicts, the Jews and Samaritans were alike in several ways. The Samaritans still valued their Israelite traditions and heritage. Their Scriptures were the five books of Moses. They also had hopes of a Messiah who would come and deliver them from being ruled by foreign governments.

During the time of Christ, there was continual conflict between Jews and Samaritans. The Jews were afraid that simply passing through Samaritan territory would make them "unclean", so they went out of their way to avoid going through Samaria. If they had to travel between Judea and Galilee, they would go east, cross over the Jordan River and travel along the river until they were near their destination, then cross back over the river.

Jesus did not avoid the Samaritans, but purposely traveled through their towns. At one time, he talked to a woman at Jacob's Well, near the Samaritan village of Sychar.

Jacob's Well

Jacob's Well (also known as Jacob's Fountain) is a deep well dug into solid rock. It has been part of the Jewish heritage for thousands of years. Today Jacob's Well is a popular tourist attraction. It is about 9 feet in diameter and about 75 feet deep. Visitors to Jacob's Well are always offered a cold drink from the well, and the water is excellent!

Review - Draw lines to match the places with the correct statements about them.

Jerusalem

Samaria

Galilee

Nazareth

Bethlehem

wilderness

Egypt

- village where Mary was visited by the angel, Gabriel
- city where Zechariah served in the Temple
- birthplace of King David and of Jesus
- where John the Baptist lived and preached
- district where Jesus talked with the woman at the well
- location of Israel's largest inland lake
- place where Joseph took his family to escape from King Herod

☐ **Checked by Tutor**   **Tutor initials** _____

Vocabulary 5

☐ **Write the meanings of these words.**
☐ **Write a sentence of your own, using each word or a form of that word.**

to avoid _____
_____

conflict _____
_____

to conquer _____
_____

constantly _____
_____

contact _____
_____

contempt _____
_____

continually _____
_____

destination _____
_____

district _____
_____

meanwhile _____
_____

normally _____
_____

policy _____
_____

purposely _____
_____

puzzled _____
_____

separate (adj) _____
_____

☐ **My student knows the meaning of these words.   Tutor initials _____**
☐ **My student has used the word correctly in a sentence.   Tutor initials _____**

29

Lesson 5 ◆ Woman at the Well

Scriptures: John 4:3-42

One day Jesus was walking with his disciples from Jerusalem to Galilee. They traveled right through Samaria. This was unusual because Jews typically avoided all contact with Samaritans.

Around noon, they came to "Jacob's Well" near one of the Samaritan villages. Jesus was tired, so he sat down to rest next to the well. His disciples went into the village to buy food.

A Samaritan woman came to the well to get water. Jesus asked her, "Will you please give me some water to drink?"

The woman was surprised. "You are a Jew, and I am a Samaritan woman. Why do you ask me for a drink, when Jews and Samaritans usually avoid each other?"

Jesus said, "You don't know the gift God has for you, and who it is you're talking to. If you did, you would ask me, and I would give you living water."

She said, "Sir, the well is deep, and you have no bucket. How can you get this 'living water'? Are you greater than Jacob who dug this well?"

Jesus said, "Those who drink from this well will get thirsty again. Those who drink my water will have a living well inside them that will continually spring up to eternal life."

The woman begged him, "Sir, please give me this water so I will never get thirsty again. Then I won't have to come back to this well."

"Go get your husband and bring him here."

"I don't have a husband."

"I know you don't. You've had five husbands, and the one you are living with now is not your husband."

"Sir, I can tell that you're a prophet. Please settle this age-old argument: We Samaritans say that this mountain is the place to worship God. The Jews say that Jerusalem is the place to worship. Who is right?"

Jesus answered, "Listen carefully. The time has now come when God is looking for those who will worship him in spirit and in truth."

The woman said, "I know that someday Messiah is coming - the one called Christ. He will explain all these things to us."

Jesus answered, "The person speaking to you is the Messiah."

About that time, the disciples came back with food. They were puzzled that Jesus was talking with the woman, but they didn't ask him about it.

The woman suddenly left her water jug behind and went into town. She told the men, "Come and see a man who told me everything I've ever done in my life. Surely, he is the Christ!"

A group of people came out of the town and asked Jesus to spend some time with them.

Meanwhile, the disciples were trying to get Jesus to eat the food they had bought. But he said to them, "I have food to eat that you know nothing about."

They looked at one another. "Did someone bring him something to eat?"

Jesus explained, "No, my food is to do the will of God and to finish his work."

Jesus stayed there for two days, and many of them believed in him as the promised Messiah. They told the woman, "It's not just because of what you told us. Now that we have heard him ourselves, we are certain that he truly is the Savior of the world!"

☐ **My student has read the story aloud.**   **Tutor initials** _____

Lesson 5 Review

☐ Fill in the blanks with the best answer.

1. Samaria was located between _____ in the north and _____ in the south.

2. The Jews around Jerusalem thought of the Samaritans as a separate _____, and they had great _____ for them.

3. Jesus did not avoid the Samaritans, but _____ traveled through their towns.

4. When Jesus was walking with his disciples from Jerusalem to Galilee, they went right through _____. They stopped at "_____ _____". Jesus was tired, so he sat down to rest while his disciples went into the village to buy food.

5. A Samaritan woman came to the well, and Jesus asked her for a _____ of water. She was _____. "You are a Jew, and I am a Samaritan woman. Why do you ask me for a drink, when Jews and Samaritans usually _____ each other?"

6. Jesus said, "You don't know the _____ God has for you, and _____ it is you are talking to. If you did, you would ask me, and I would give you _____ water."

7. She said, "Sir, the well is deep, and you have no _____. How can you get this 'living water'? Are you greater than Jacob who dug this well?"

8. Jesus said, "Those who drink from this well will get _____ again. Those who drink my water will have a living well inside them that will _____ spring up to eternal life."

9. Jesus told the woman, ". . .God is looking for those who will worship him in _____ and in _____." She said, "I know that someday Messiah is coming - the one called _____."

10. Jesus answered, "The person speaking to you is the _____."

11. About that time, the disciples came back with food. They were _____ that Jesus was talking with the woman, but they didn't ask him about it.

12. The woman suddenly left her water jug behind and went into _____. She told the men, "Come and see a man who told me everything I've ever done in my life. _____, he is the Christ!"

13. A group of people came from the town and asked Jesus to _____ some time with them.

14. Jesus stayed there for two days, and many of them _____ that he was the Messiah.

15. They told the woman, "It's not just because of what you told us. Now that we have heard him ourselves, we are _____ that he truly is the _____ of the world!"

☐ Checked by Tutor   Tutor initials _____

☐ My student has told the story aloud in his/her own words.   Tutor initials _____   31

Reflection and Questions
Lesson 5 ◈ Woman at the Well

☐ Read the questions on this page.
☐ Tell your thoughts aloud or write your answers on the next page.

Your perspective:

- Tell about a time when an important person took time to visit with you.

- When a stranger starts talking to you, how do you know if they are honest and genuine?

- Tell about a time when you were enjoying a conversation so much that you "forgot to eat."

Review the facts:

- Where was Jesus when he talked to the woman? What time of day was it?

- What questions did the woman ask Jesus, and how did he answer each one?

Search for answers:

- What factors influenced the Samaritans to believe that Jesus was the Messiah?

Writing assignments:

- Imagine you are the Samaritan woman. Write your thoughts about what happened and about how your life will be different from now on.

- Explain the meaning of *living water* based on the following Scriptures:
    Psalm 36:9   Jeremiah 2:13

Final thoughts:

- What do you think caused the woman to believe that Jesus was the Messiah?

- If you lived in the time of Jesus, what might make you believe that someone was a true "prophet of God"?

- How do you think a person can worship God "in spirit and in truth"?

Notes

 # Background History for Lesson 6

The Beatitudes

The beginning section of the *Sermon on the Mount* is called the "Beatitudes", meaning *supreme blessedness*. In this section of the sermon, Jesus described the character qualities of those who are *blessed*. He taught that people are blessed by God, even though their circumstances may look the opposite from an earthly perspective.

The Kingdom of Heaven

The terms 'kingdom of heaven' and 'kingdom of God' are both used in the *New Testament*. These words refer to the work of God—his kingly rule and the fact that he governs the whole universe.

The people of Israel were expecting a different kind of kingdom. They thought Jesus was going to restore the Kingdom of David. They expected him to deliver them from the Romans and make Israel an independent nation once again.

The Law

There are 613 commandments in the Law of Moses. These are divided into three parts: moral, religious and civil laws. When the *New Testament* refers to "the Law", it could mean one of several things. It might mean the Law of Moses (first five books of the Scriptures); it could be referring to the Law of Moses plus the *Psalms* and the *Prophets;* or it could mean the entire *Old Testament*.

How Jesus fulfilled the Law of God

1) He fulfilled its prophecies about the Messiah. The Scriptures prophesied (foretold) his birth, life, and death.

2) Jesus respected the Law of Moses. He quoted from it throughout his ministry.

3) Jesus always obeyed the Law of God. The religious leaders constantly searched for a time when he broke the law, but they couldn't find any time when that happened.

4) The death of Jesus fulfilled God's requirement of a sacrifice for sin.

Quick Definitions

lust: to have a strong desire for someone or something

mercy: kindness, forgiveness, or help given to someone

murder: the crime of purposely killing a person

righteous: doing right

seek: looking for; trying to get or find

narrow: small from one side to the other; tight; opposite of wide

wide: having a large amount of distance from one side to the other

---

Vocabulary 6

☐ **Write the meanings of these words.**

☐ **Write a sentence of your own, using each word or a form of that word.**

to beware _____

character quality _____

circumstances _____

commandments _____

to commit adultery _____

destruction _____

foundation _____

generous _____

to judge _____

to marvel _____

privately _____

to restore _____

standard _____

treasures _____

to treat _____

☐ **My student knows the meaning of these words.   Tutor initials** _____

☐ **My student has used the word correctly in a sentence.   Tutor initials** _____

35

Lesson 6 ❖ Sermon on the Mount

Scriptures: Matt 5:1-44, Matt 6:1-33, Matt 7:1-29, Luke 6:20-49, Exodus 21:24

The Beatitudes

Jesus went up on a mountain to teach. He explained what it takes to be a disciple of Messiah and how to live a life that is pleasing to God. He said:

- Blessed are the poor in spirit, because the kingdom of heaven is theirs.

- Blessed are those who mourn, because they will be comforted.

- Blessed are the gentle, because they will inherit the earth.

- Blessed are those who hunger and thirst for righteousness, because they will be filled.

- Blessed are the merciful, because they will receive mercy.

- Blessed are the pure in heart, because they will see God.

- Blessed are the peacemakers, because they will be known as the children of God.

- Blessed are those who are persecuted for righteousness, because the kingdom of heaven is theirs.

- Blessed are you when people insult you and persecute you because of me. Rejoice and be exceedingly glad, because great is your reward in heaven. That is how they persecuted the prophets who came before you.

If you do these things, you will be the salt of the earth. You will be the light of the world. People will see it and give praise to God.

A Higher Standard

Jesus continued speaking. "Don't think that I have come to get rid of the Law of God. Just the opposite! My disciples should live by a higher standard.

The Law says you are not to murder. I am giving you a higher standard. You are not to hate anyone. When you hate a person it is as bad as killing them.

The Law says you are not to commit adultery. I'm giving you a higher standard. You are not to keep lust in your heart.

The Law says 'an eye for an eye, a tooth for a tooth.' You should live at a higher standard. If someone does something bad to you, do something good for them. If you do these things, blessings will come back on you!"

Warnings

Jesus talked about things that keep people from serving God the way they should.

(1) "Beware of pride—trying to impress people instead of God. When you give to the poor, do it privately. Don't try to show off how generous you are. When you pray, just talk to God. It's not a time to show off. Do these things privately. God will reward you.

(2) Beware of the control money can have over you. Don't work to have great treasures on earth, but work to have treasures in heaven. For where your treasure is, there will your heart be also.

You can't serve two masters. You will either serve God and use money to honor him, or you will be controlled by money and what it can buy you.

Ask, and it shall be given to you; seek, and you shall find; knock, and it shall be opened unto you. Trust God, and he will take care of you.

(3) Don't worry! You need food and clothing, but you shouldn't worry about them. Look at the birds and see how God provides food for them. Don't you think he cares more for you? Look how he 'dresses' the wild flowers. They are even more beautiful than when King Solomon was wearing his finest royal robes! God knows what you need, and he will take care of you. Don't worry about tomorrow. Each day has enough trouble of its own.

(4) Beware of judging other people. You will be judged by the standards you set for others. Forgive others, and others will forgive you. Give to others, and others will give to you. Treat others exactly the way you want them to treat you."

Conclusion

Jesus said, "If you want to be my disciples, then listen to what I say, and do it. There are two roads before you. One is wide and well traveled. It is the easy way, and most people use it, but it leads to destruction. The other road is narrow, and only a few people find it. It is the hard way, but it leads to life.

It is like two men who built houses for themselves. One made his foundation on a rock. The other man built his house on sand. Then the storms came and beat on both houses. The house on the rock stood firm, and the other house was totally destroyed.

Build your life upon the firm foundation of what I am teaching you. If you do, you will be strong when the 'storms of life' come upon you."

When Jesus finished teaching, the people marvelled! He taught them with complete authority.

☐ **My student has read the story aloud.**   **Tutor initials** _____

Lesson 6 Review

☐ Fill in the blanks with the best answer.

1. Jesus went up on a mountain to teach. He explained what it takes to
   be a _____ of Messiah, and how to live a life that is _____ to God.

2. Jesus said, "If you do these things, you will be the _____ of the earth. You will be the
   _____ of the world. People will see it and give _____ to God."

3. Jesus said, "Don't think that I have come to get rid of the Law of God. Just the opposite! My
   disciples should live by a _____ standard.

4. The Law says you are not to _____ . . . I say, you are not to _____ anyone. When
   you hate a person it is as bad as killing them.

5. The Law says you are not to commit _____ . . . I say, you are not to keep lust in
   your _____ .

6. The Law says 'an eye for an eye, a tooth for a tooth.' I say . . . if someone does something _____
   to you, do something _____ for them.

7. Beware of pride—trying to _____ people instead of God.

8. When you give to the poor, do it privately. Don't show off how _____ you are.

9. Don't work to have great _____ on earth, but work to have treasures in _____ .
   You can't serve two masters. You will either serve _____ and use money to honor him, or you
   will be _____ by money and what it can buy you.

10. Ask, and it shall be _____ to you; seek, and you shall _____ ; knock, and it shall be
    _____ unto you. Trust God, and he will take care of you.

11. Don't worry! You need food and clothing, but you shouldn't _____ about them. God
    knows what you _____ , and he will take care of you.

12. Beware of _____ other people. You will be judged by the _____ you
    set for others.

13. Forgive others, and others will _____ you. Give to others, and others will give to you.
    Treat others _____ the way you want them to _____ you.

14. There are two roads before you. One is _____ and well traveled. It is the easy way, and most
    people use it, but it leads to _____ . The other road is narrow, and only a
    few people find it. It is the hard way, but it leads to _____ .

15. Build your life upon the firm _____ of what I am teaching you. If you do,
    you will be strong when the '_____ of life' come upon you."

16. When Jesus finished teaching, the people _____ ! He taught them with
    complete _____ .

☐ Checked by Tutor   Tutor initials _____   37

Reflection and Questions
Lesson 6 ◈ Sermon on the Mount

☐ Read the questions on this page.
☐ Tell your thoughts aloud or write your answers on the next page.

Your perspective:

- What are some wise sayings from your culture that tell how a person can be happy?

- What "treasures" do most people dream of having?

- What things in your daily life tend to worry you the most?

- Tell about a person who "judged" someone else and later found out they were mistaken?

- Give an example of when you helped someone in need, and then someone else gave to you.

Review the facts:

- Tell the two examples Jesus used to explain why people should trust God and not worry about food and clothes.

- What was the response of the people who heard Jesus teach?

Search for answers:

- Look over the Beatitudes and tell five character qualities that can help a person be happy.

Writing assignments:

- Choose one of the "Beatitudes" and tell why it is meaningful to you.

- List three sayings in today's world that are based on the ideas taught in this sermon.

- What advice would you give to help children build their lives on a good foundation?

Final thoughts:

- What is the meaning of "an eye for an eye and a tooth for a tooth"? How should our lives be different than that?

- What does it mean to be the "salt of the earth" or the "light of the world"?

- How do you think a person can have "treasures in heaven"?

- What statements from the Sermon on the Mount are most meaningful to you? Tell why.

- Give an example from today's world that illustrates the idea of a "wide road" that leads to a bad result, as compared to a "narrow road" that leads to a good result.

- Jesus referred to the "storms of life." What are some "storms of life" in today's world?

- What is one way you can be a 'peacemaker'?

Notes

Background History for Lesson 7

The Sea of Galilee

The Sea of Galilee is Israel's largest inland lake. It is 650 feet below sea level, making it the world's lowest fresh-water lake. It is about 13 miles long and 7 miles wide. It is also called the Sea of Tiberias or Lake Genneseret.

The earthly ministry of Jesus centered around the Sea of Galilee. Although he did go to Jerusalem for some occasions, the Lord spent most of the three years of his ministry along the shore of the Sea of Galilee.

The Sea of Galilee is known for its violent storms, which can come up very suddenly. These are caused because of its having steep hills on all sides. Cooler air from the surrounding mountains mixes with warm air in the lake's basin. Wind funnels are formed that rush down the hillsides by the lake, creating very rough water.

Capernaum

This town was a fishing village on the northwestern shore of the Sea of Galilee. There were other fishing villages all around the lake, but Capernaum became the headquarters for Christ's Galilean ministry. While in that area, he probably stayed at Peter's house much of the time.

Evil Spirits

At one time, Satan was a high-ranking angel named Lucifer. He started a rebellion that involved one-third of all the angels. Satan and his angels were thrown out of heaven. He became known as the *devil,* and his angels became *evil spirits* — also called *unclean spirits.*

Evil spirits are living beings which do not have bodies, so they constantly seek to live inside another body—human or animal. They serve the devil, fighting against anything that is good.

Evil spirits hate humans because people were made by God, in the 'image of God'. We were made for his pleasure. Therefore, evil spirits work against people, always bringing great suffering.

The Scripture says that an eternal fire is prepared for the devil and his angels. They know they will eventually be thrown into hell where they will be tormented for all eternity. Because of this, they fear Jesus.

Part of Jesus' ministry on earth was to "cast out" evil spirits. That is, he ordered them to leave a person's body. When Jesus confronted them, they always obeyed him because they knew who he was and they recognized his power and authority.

Vocabulary 7

☐ **Write the meanings of these words.**

☐ **Write a sentence of your own, using each word or a form of that word.**

approval _____

_____

captivated (adj) _____

_____

confidence _____

_____

to confront _____

_____

eventually _____

_____

injured _____

_____

neighboring _____

_____

partners _____

_____

rebellion _____

_____

to recognize _____

_____

rough _____

_____

to scream _____

_____

solitary _____

_____

to torment _____

_____

violent _____

_____

☐ **My student knows the meaning of these words.   Tutor initials _____**

☐ **My student has used the word correctly in a sentence.   Tutor initials _____**

Lesson 7 ◈ Fishing for People

Scriptures: Mark 1:22-38, Luke 4:31-44, Luke 5:1-11, Matthew 8:14-17

In the Synagogue

Jesus went to the synagogue in Capernaum. There he taught the people, and they were totally captivated by his message. Jesus wasn't like other teachers of the law; he didn't look for approval from the religious leaders. He taught with complete confidence and authority.

One time, while he was teaching, a man was there who had an evil spirit in him. When he saw Jesus, the spirit shouted, "Leave us alone! Have you come to destroy us? I know who you are! You are the Holy One of God."

Jesus looked at the man. Then he ordered the spirit, "Don't speak. Come out of him!"

The evil spirit threw the man onto the floor. He screamed as the spirit violently left his body, but he was not injured.

Those who stood by were amazed! They said, "Even the evil spirits obey him!" After this event, the fame of Jesus spread everywhere around Galilee.

At Peter's House

Afterwards, Jesus went with James and John to the home of Peter and his brother Andrew. Peter's mother-in-law was sick in bed with a high fever. They asked Jesus to heal her, so he went to where she was lying, reached out and took her hand. Immediately, the fever left her, and she got up. She was completely recovered, so she started serving her guests.

By that evening, almost the entire town was there at her house. Jesus taught the people, healed the sick, and cast out evil spirits.

A Solitary Place

The next morning, Jesus got up early—even before the sun was up. He went out to a solitary place where he could be alone and pray. When everyone else in the town woke up, Peter and his friends went to look for Jesus. When they finally found him, they said, "Everyone is looking for you!"

Jesus replied, "I must go to the neighboring towns so I can preach there also. That is why I was sent to earth. So Jesus and his disciples traveled throughout Galilee, teaching, healing, and casting out evil spirits.

At the Sea of Galilee

One day Jesus went to the shore of the Sea of Galilee to teach the people. They crowded closely around so they could hear him speak.

Jesus got into one of the fishing boats that was pulled up to the shore. It was owned by Peter. Jesus asked him to push off from shore a little. Once this was done, he sat down and taught the people.

After he finished teaching, Jesus said to Peter, "Go out into deeper water and let out the nets."

Peter said, "Lord, we have been fishing all night and haven't caught anything. Still, if that is what you want, I will let out a net." He then took the boat out into deeper water and let out a net. Immediately, he caught a huge number of fish—so many—that the net started breaking. Peter called out, "James, John!" His fishing partners came with their boat and helped bring in the fish. They filled both boats until they were in danger of sinking.

Peter saw this miracle and then fell to his knees and said, "Oh, Lord, please leave me! I'm too much of a sinner for you to be around me."

Jesus said, "Don't be afraid. In the past you have caught fish. From now on, your work will be catching people!"

The fishing partners—Peter, James, and John—pulled their boats up on the shore. Then, they left everything, and became disciples of Jesus.

☐ **My student has read the story aloud.**   **Tutor initials** _____

Lesson 7 Review

☐ **Fill in the blanks with the best answer.**

1. When Jesus taught the people, they were totally _____ by his message.

2. Jesus wasn't like other teachers of the law; he didn't look for _____ from the religious leaders. He taught with complete _____ and authority.

3. One day, while Jesus was teaching, a man was there who had an _____ _____ in him. The spirit shouted, "Leave us alone! Have you come to _____ us?"

4. Jesus _____ the spirit, "Don't speak. Come out of him!"

5. The evil spirit _____ him onto the floor. The man screamed as the spirit _____ left his body, but he was not _____. Those who stood by were amazed! They said, "Even the evil spirits obey him!"

6. After this event, the _____ of Jesus spread everywhere around Galilee.

7. Jesus went with James and John to the home of _____ and his brother _____. Peter's mother-in-law was sick in bed with a high _____.

8. They asked Jesus to _____ her, so he went to where she was lying, reached out and _____ her hand. Immediately, the fever left her, and she got up. She was completely _____, so she started _____ her guests.

9. The next morning, Jesus woke up early and went out to a _____ place where he could be alone and pray. Peter and his _____ went to look for Jesus. Eventually, they found him and said, "_____ is looking for you!"

10. Jesus replied, "I must go to the _____ towns so I can preach there also."

11. So, Jesus and his disciples traveled _____ the area of Galilee, teaching, healing, and casting out evil spirits.

12. One day Jesus taught from a _____ boat that was pulled up to the shore. When he finished teaching, Jesus said to Peter, "Go out into deeper water and let out the _____."

13. Peter said, "Lord, we have been fishing all _____ and haven't caught anything. But if that's what you want, I will let out a net." He took the boat out into deep water and let out a _____.

14. Immediately, he caught a huge number of fish—so many—that the net started _____.

15. His fishing partners came and helped bring in the fish. They filled _____ boats until they were in _____ of sinking.

16. Peter saw this miracle, then fell to his knees and said, "Oh, Lord, please _____ me! I'm too much of a _____ for you to be around me."

17. Jesus said, "Don't be afraid. In the past you have _____ fish. From now on, your work will be catching _____!" Peter, James, and John pulled their boats up on the shore. Then they _____ everything, and became _____ of Jesus.

☐ **Checked by Tutor   Tutor initials** _____

☐ **My student has told the story aloud in his/her own words.   Tutor initials** _____

Reflection and Questions
Lesson 7 ❖ Fishing for People

❑ Read the questions on this page.
❑ Tell your thoughts aloud or write your answers on the next page.

Your perspective:

- What did people mean when they said Jesus spoke with confidence and authority? Name some people you know who are like this.

- Tell about someone who makes you feel like spending more time with them. What are some good qualities of that person?

Review the facts:

- Name at least four different locations (places) mentioned in this lesson.

Search for answers:

- Tell three ways in which Jesus showed his authority and power.

- What reason did Peter give for asking the Lord to leave him?

Writing assignments:

- Describe a "solitary place" where you like to go and be alone.

Final thoughts:

- Jesus told Peter, "From now on you will be catching people." What do you think he meant?

- Why do you think the fishermen were willing to leave their way of life and become disciples of Jesus?

Notes

Background History for Lesson 8

Welcoming Guests

Certain customs were observed when a guest was invited into a Jewish home.

A person's feet would be hot and dusty after walking along the road in sandals. He would remove his sandals before entering a home.

A polite host showed respect to an honored guest by providing water for washing his feet. Normally, a maid-servant would do the job, but it was an act of great humility and affection if the host himself washed the feet of his guest.

It was customary to greet friends entering the home with a kiss on each cheek. A host could also show respect to an honored guest by pouring perfumed oil on his head.

The meal was served on a low table. On special occasions, Jewish people followed the Greek and Roman custom of reclining on their left side and leaning on a cushion with their left elbow, while eating with their right hand. Their heads were toward the table and their feet were stretched out behind.

Review Quotes - Draw lines to match the people with what they said.

Zechariah

Elizabeth

The angel, Gabriel

Herod the King

angels who visited shepherds

wise men from the east

Satan

Nicodemus

John the Baptist

Jesus

woman at the well

disciples of Jesus

Peter

A ruler from Capernaum

• Your child will be the son of God.

• Where is the child who has been born to be King of the Jews?

• How am I worthy to have the mother of my Lord visit me?

• Glory to God in the highest! Peace and good will to the earth.

• Come back and let me know, so I can go and worship him, too.

• You, my son, will prepare the way for Messiah.

• My food is to do the will of God, and to finish his work.

• Make these stones into bread.

• We know you are from God because we see your miracles.

• Don't you care that we are going to die?

• Lord, please leave me. I'm too much of a sinner!

• Please come and heal my son, or he will die!

• Come and see a man who told me everything I ever did.

• Here comes the Lamb of God who takes away the sin of the world!

☐ Checked by Tutor   Tutor initials _____

Vocabulary 8

☐ Write the meanings of these words.
☐ Write a sentence of your own, using each word or a form of that word.

absolutely _____

_____

blasphemy _____

_____

debt _____

_____

expensive _____

_____

grateful _____

_____

gratitude _____

_____

horrified _____

_____

neither _____

_____

ordinary _____

_____

overflowing _____

_____

paralyzed _____

_____

polite _____

_____

sinner _____

_____

to stretch out _____

_____

to suppose _____

_____

☐ My student knows the meaning of these words.   Tutor initials _____

☐ My student has used the word correctly in a sentence.   Tutor initials _____

Lesson 8 ◆ Forgiving Sins

Scriptures: Mark 2:1-12, Luke 5:17-26, Luke 7:36-50

A Paralyzed Man and Four Friends

At Capernaum, Jesus went into a house to teach. When word got out that he was there, the house was soon filled to overflowing! People were standing in the doorway and outside the house. Some religious rulers were also there.

Four men came, carrying a paralyzed man on a cot. They quickly realized that there was no ordinary way to get into the house. So they carried the man on his cot up the outside stairs to the roof of the house. There they made an opening in the roof by removing the tiles. When it was big enough they lowered the man down into the middle of the crowd, in front of Jesus.

When Jesus saw the faith of the four men, he turned and said to the man lying on the cot, "Son, your sins are forgiven."

The religious rulers were horrified! They thought to themselves, *How dare this man say such things! He is speaking blasphemy! Only God can forgive sins.*

Jesus knew what they were thinking, so he said, "Why are you so troubled in your thoughts? I could have easily said, 'Get up and walk,' but you needed to know that I have the authority to forgive sins."

Then he said to the man, "Get up, pick up your cot, and go home."

Immediately the man got up, picked up his cot, and walked out in front of them all. People in the crowd were amazed! They gave praise to God, saying, "We have never seen anything like this before!"

Washing the Feet of Jesus

A Pharisee named Simon invited Jesus to come to his house for a meal. Their custom was to lean on a cushion next to the table, with their feet stretched out behind.

While they were eating, a woman—who was known to be a great sinner—walked in, carrying a jar of expensive perfumed oil. She stood behind Jesus, next to his feet. Then she bowed her head and began to cry. She cried so much that her tears were falling on the feet of Jesus.

She knelt on the floor, let down her hair, and used it to dry his feet. Then she kissed them and poured oil on them.

Simon thought to himself, *This proves that Jesus is not a prophet. If he were, he would know what kind of woman she is and not let her touch him.*

Forgiven and Grateful

Jesus knew what Simon was thinking. He said, "Simon, there's something I want to say to you."

Simon answered, "Go ahead and say it, Teacher."

> 'Denarii' is plural for 'denarius' which was a Roman coin, the average amount of a day's wages for a skilled laborer.

Jesus told Simon this story: "Two men owed a debt to the same banker. One owed 50 denarii while the other owed 500 denarii. Neither of them could pay what they owed, which meant that they would be taken into slavery. Instead, the banker decided to forgive their debt and set them free. Now, my question for you—which of these men will be more grateful to the banker?"

Simon was quick to answer. "I suppose, the one to whom he forgave the most."

Jesus said, "You are absolutely right!" I came into your house and you did not give me any water for washing my feet. Look at this woman. She didn't say a word, but simply washed my feet with her tears and dried them with her hair. When I came to your house, you did not welcome me with a customary kiss, but she has not stopped kissing my feet. You didn't offer me any oil with which to freshen up. She has poured perfume on my feet.

Why has she done all these things? It is because her sins are many, and she is so grateful to be forgiven! People who feel they've been good all their lives will not experience such deep gratitude."

He turned to the woman. "Your sins are forgiven." This shocked those sitting around the table. Then Jesus said to her, "Your faith has saved you; go in peace."

☐ **My student has read the story aloud.**   **Tutor initials** _____

Lesson 8 Review

☐ Fill in the blanks with the best answer.

1. At Capernaum, Jesus went into a house to teach. When word got out that

   he was there, the house was soon filled to _____!

2. Four men came, carrying a _____ man on a cot. Since there was no _____

   way to get into the house, they carried the man on his cot up to the roof of the house. There they

   made an opening in the roof and _____ the man down in front of Jesus.

3. When Jesus saw the _____ of the four men, he turned and said to the man lying on the cot,

   "Son, your sins are _____."

4. The religious rulers were _____! They thought, *He is speaking blasphemy! Only*

   God can forgive sins. Jesus knew what they were thinking, so he said, "I could have easily said,

   'Get up and walk,' but you needed to know that I have the _____ to forgive sins."

5. Jesus said to the man, "Get up, pick up your _____, and go home." And he did! The people in

   the crowd gave _____ to God, saying, "We've never seen anything like this before!"

6. A _____ named Simon invited Jesus to come to his house for a meal.

7. While they were eating, a woman came in and stood _____ Jesus, next to his feet. Then

   she began to _____. Her tears were falling on the feet of Jesus. She knelt on the floor and

   used her _____ to dry his feet. Then she kissed them and poured oil on them.

8. Simon _____ to himself, *This proves that Jesus is not a prophet. If he were, he would*

   know what _____ of woman she is and not let her _____ him.

9. Jesus told Simon this _____: "Two men _____ a debt to the same banker. One owed

   50 denarii while the other owed 500 denarii. _____ of them could pay what they owed,

   which meant that they would be taken into _____. Instead, the banker decided to

   _____ their debt and set them free.

10. Then Jesus asked, "Now, which of these men will be more _____ to the banker?"

11. Simon was quick to answer. "I _____, the one to whom he forgave the _____."

12. Jesus said, "You are _____ right! Why has this woman done all these things?

    It is because her _____ are many, and she is so grateful to be _____! People

    who feel they've been good all their lives will not experience such deep _____."

13. He turned to the woman, "Your sins are forgiven." This _____ those sitting around

    the table. Then Jesus said to her, "Your faith has _____ you; go in peace."

☐ **Checked by Tutor**   **Tutor initials** _____

☐ **My student has told the story aloud in his/her own words.**   **Tutor initials** _____   49

Reflection and Questions
Lesson 8 ◇ Forgiving Sins

❑ **Read the questions on this page.**
❑ **Tell your thoughts aloud or write your answers on the next page.**

Your perspective:

- Tell about an occasion where you spent time with friends and had a special meal together.

- What are some of your customs for welcoming guests into your home?

- What are some of your customs for eating a meal together?

- Tell about a time when someone helped a person in need, but others did not like it.

Review the facts:

- Describe the two people in this lesson whose sins were forgiven by Jesus.

- What unusual method did the men use to bring the paralyzed man to Jesus?

Search for answers:

- Describe the kind of people who became upset when Jesus said,
  "Your sins are forgiven" or "Your faith has saved you."

- Why were people shocked when Jesus told someone that their sins were forgiven?

Writing assignments:

- List the character qualities Jesus showed as he spoke to:
  (1) the paralyzed man
  (2) his four friends
  (3) Simon the Pharisee,
  (4) the woman who poured perfumed oil on his feet.

Final thoughts:

- Why do you think it is so important for people to have their sins forgiven?

Notes

My student's English grammar and sentence structure is correct.   Tutor initials _____

# Background History for Lesson 9

The Sabbath

The Jewish sabbath was the last day of the week—a day of rest when no work was to be done. Many Pharisees believed that Messiah would not come until all of Israel kept the sabbath law perfectly just once. This made them feel extremely worried about keeping the Sabbath. They made a long list of things they felt were not allowed on that day. These were not actually in the Law of God, but their rules became a tradition among the Jews.

One thing on the list was a rule about how far a person could travel on the Sabbath. A 'Sabbath day's journey' was about 1,000 yards (914 meters) beyond the city walls.

Eating Together

Having a meal with someone is an important symbol around the world. It is a common human thought that sharing food with someone is sharing life with them. In most cultures, eating with someone creates a bond of fellowship. During the time of Christ, sharing a meal was a sign of friendship and community.

The Jews felt that eating together was also a religious experience. It was a way to celebrate their faith, and it included many rules about what happened around the table. They were to have clean food, clean dishes, clean hands, and clean hearts. A proper Jewish meal was a way for believers to worship God during an everyday occasion in their lives.

Tax Collectors and Sinners

The Roman government ruled over Israel during the time of Christ. Taxes on Jewish families totaled about one-third of their annual income. This money was used to pay Roman soldiers and to pay for the Romans' many construction projects.

Jewish tax collectors were called *publicans* because they were employees of the Roman government and collected public funds. Jewish people hated publicans, and thought of them as traitors. To make things worse, tax collectors were allowed to collect more than the actual amount that people owed. Many publicans became rich by greatly overcharging the people and keeping the extra money for themselves!

- In Israel, tax collectors could not hold political positions in their communities.

- They were not allowed to give testimony in Jewish courts.

- They were not welcome at social events.

- They were regarded on the same social level as robbers, adulterers, and other evildoers.

- Some religious leaders said it was impossible for tax collectors to genuinely repent, since they could not possibly give back all the extra money they had taken from others.

- The only friends of tax collectors were people who were social outcasts like themselves. Therefore, Matthew invited "tax collectors and sinners" to his house.

Vocabulary 9

☐ Write the meanings of these words.
☐ Write a sentence of your own, using each word or a form of that word.

crippled _____

_____

to criticize _____

_____

everyday _____

_____

fellowship _____

_____

to host _____

_____

to infuriate _____

_____

legal _____

_____

loyal _____

_____

to overcharge _____

_____

political _____

_____

reputation _____

_____

to share _____

_____

social outcast _____

_____

traitor _____

_____

wolf/wolves _____

_____

☐ My student knows the meaning of these words.   Tutor initials _____

☐ My student has used the word correctly in a sentence.   Tutor initials _____   53

Lesson 9 ◈ Healing and Teaching

Scriptures: Luke 6:6-16, Mark 3:1-6, Matt. 9:9-13, Matt.10:1-39, Matt.12:9-14

Healing a Crippled Hand

Once again, Jesus went into a synagogue to teach. Many people gathered around to listen to him. In the crowd, was a man with a crippled hand.

Some of the Pharisees and teachers of the law were there, too. They had come because they thought this might be their opportunity to catch Jesus breaking God's Law. The Old Testament taught that a person was not supposed to work on the Sabbath. They felt Jesus was working when he healed someone. So, they asked him, "Is it legal to heal on the Sabbath?"

Jesus knew what they were thinking. He told the man with a crippled hand, "Get up and stand here." So, he got up and stood in front of them all.

Jesus then turned to the religious leaders and said, "I have a question for you. Is it legal to do good on the Sabbath, or to do evil? Is it better to save life or destroy it?" They did not answer him.

Jesus continued talking, "If you had a sheep that fell into a pit on the Sabbath, you would not hesitate to pull it out. A person is better than a sheep! Therefore I will answer the question. Yes, it is absolutely legal to do good on the Sabbath."

He then turned to the man and said, "Stretch out your hand."

The man stretched out his hand, and when he did, it was healed and became as strong as his other one.

This infuriated the religious rulers! They immediately began to discuss among themselves how they could kill Jesus.

Matthew

Jesus was walking toward the seashore. Along the way he saw a tax collector named Matthew sitting at a tax booth. Jesus stopped and said to him, "Matthew, follow me." Immediately, Matthew left everything and followed Jesus.

Soon afterwards, Matthew hosted a meal for Jesus in his house. He invited many other tax collectors. They came, as well as various people of low reputation.

Once again, the religious leaders criticized Jesus. They asked his disciples, "Why is your Master eating with tax collectors and sinners?"

Jesus heard what they said, so he answered them. "Doctors are for people who are sick, not for people who are well. I have not come to help people who think they are righteous. I am calling sinners to repent."

Calling Twelve Disciples

One evening, Jesus left the crowd and went up on a mountain to be alone and pray. He prayed the entire night.

At daybreak, he came down from the mountain and chose a small group of twelve men from among his followers—disciples to work closely with him. These men would stay with him so he could teach them and prepare them to preach. He gave them power to heal the sick and cast out evil spirits.

Sending Out the Twelve

Jesus sent his disciples out to teach the people. He said, "I am sending you out like sheep among wolves. Therefore, be as wise as snakes, yet as harmless as doves.

People will hate you just like they have hated me, but don't be afraid. Your Heavenly Father is watching over you. He knows when a sparrow falls to the ground, and you are more valuable than a sparrow. He has even counted the hairs on your head.

Members of your family will want you to be loyal to them instead of being loyal to me. If you choose their approval, you are not worthy of me.

If you live your life without me, you will lose it; and if you lose your life because of me, you will actually find it."

☐ **My student has read the story aloud.**   **Tutor initials** _____

Lesson 9 Review

☐ **Fill in the blanks with the best answer.**

1. The Jewish _____ was the last day of the week—a day of rest when people were not supposed to _____.

2. The Pharisees made a list of things they felt were not allowed on that day. These were _____ actually in the Law of God, but they still became a _____ among the Jews.

3. Jesus was teaching in a synagogue, and in the crowd was a man with a _____ hand.

4. Some religious leaders came because they thought this might be their opportunity to _____ Jesus breaking God's law. They asked, "Is it _____ to heal on the Sabbath?"

5. Jesus knew what they were _____ , so he told the man with a crippled hand, "Get up and stand here."

6. Jesus then turned to the _____ leaders and asked, "Is it legal to do _____ on the Sabbath, or to do _____? Is it better to _____ life or _____ it?" They did not _____ him.

7. He turned to the man and said, "_____ out your hand!" The man did so, and his hand was healed; it became as _____ as his other one.

8. This _____ the religious rulers! They immediately began to _____ among themselves how they could kill Jesus.

9. Matthew (who had been a tax collector) _____ a meal for Jesus in his house. He invited other tax collectors, as well as various people of low _____.

10. Once again, the religious leaders _____ Jesus. They asked his disciples, "_____ is your Master eating with tax collectors and sinners?"

11. Jesus heard what they said, so he answered. "Doctors are for people who are _____, not for people who are _____. I have not come to help people who think they are _____. I am calling sinners to repent."

12. Jesus sent twelve disciples out to teach the people. He said, "I am sending you out like _____ among _____. Therefore, be as wise as snakes, yet as harmless as doves.

13. People will _____ you just like they have hated me, but don't be _____.

14. Your Heavenly Father is watching over you. He knows when a _____ falls to the ground, and you are more _____ than a sparrow.

15. Members of your _____ will want you to be loyal to them instead of being _____ to me. If you choose their _____ , you are not worthy of me.

16. If you live your life without me, you will _____ it; and if you lose your life because of me, you will actually _____ it."

☐ **Checked by Tutor   Tutor initials** _____

☐ **My student has told the story aloud in his/her own words.   Tutor initials** _____   55

Reflection and Questions
Lesson 9 ◈ Healing and Teaching

❑ Read the questions on this page.
❑ Tell your thoughts aloud or write your answers on the next page.

Your perspective:

- Describe a time when you chose to give up doing something you enjoyed in order to do something more important.

- Tell about a time when you did something good and you "got in trouble" for doing it.

- How would you describe the type of people who became angry when Jesus healed or forgave someone?

Review the facts:

- What kind of people most often criticized Jesus?

Search for answers:

- What does it mean to be "like sheep among wolves"?

- What does it mean to be "as wise as serpents and harmless as doves"?

Writing assignments:

- Write three statements Jesus made to his disciples that are meaningful to you.

- Write three modern sayings that are based on what Jesus taught.

Final thoughts:

- Why do you think the religious officials become angry with Jesus for healing someone?

- Jesus said, "If you live your life without me, you will lose it; and if you lose your life because of me, you will actually find it." Give an example of this truth.

Notes

Background History for Lesson 10

Parables

Storytelling is a powerful means of teaching. Jewish rabbis have used stories down through the years to communicate their traditions and values.

A parable is a simple story that is told for the purpose of teaching a lesson. Parables require people to pay attention and listen carefully in order to interpret the meaning. It is important to understand how the parable relates to the real message that the speaker is trying to get across.

Large crowds gathered around Jesus as he taught them with parables. These stories were based on everyday things that were part of the life experience of the listeners.

Many of the parables were based on the setting of fishermen, shepherds, and farmers. Some were about kings and their citizens, or masters and their servants. When his disciples did not understand the meaning, Jesus explained the stories to them.

The parables of Jesus helped his listeners understand spiritual concepts and make an informed decision whether or not to follow Christ. The crowds were so captivated by his teaching that Jesus often had to "send the people away" when he was finished speaking.

The Other Side of the Sea of Galilee

Jesus grew up in Nazareth, about twenty miles west of the Sea of Galilee. He spent a lot of his time in that area. The towns of Capernaum, Tiberias, and Magdala were all on the west side of the Sea of Galilee—the Jewish side.

"The other side" was the Gentile side of the lake, the eastern shore of the Sea of Galilee. In Lesson 10, you will read how Jesus and his disciples crossed the lake and landed in the region of Decapolis, a Greek name meaning *ten cities*. This was the first time Jesus took his disciples into Gentile territory.

After the wild man from among the tombs was healed, he wanted to go with Jesus and his disciples to the Jewish side of the lake. But, he didn't get to do that. Jesus told him to go home to his friends and family and tell them what God had done for him.

For the next year and a half, the man traveled throughout Decapolis telling people about Jesus. He became the first Gentile missionary to the Gentiles.

The next time Jesus came to the region of Decapolis, there were 4,000 Gentile believers, waiting to greet him and listen to him speak. *(Mark 7:31-37, Mark 8:1-9)*

Vocabulary 10

☐ Write the meanings of these words.

☐ Write a sentence of your own, using each word or a form of that word.

to choke out _____

_____

cliff _____

_____

to communicate _____

_____

to drown _____

_____

informed decision _____

_____

to interpret _____

_____

missionary _____

_____

to pay attention _____

_____

persecution _____

_____

pleasure _____

_____

possessed _____

_____

region _____

_____

to relate _____

_____

to scatter _____

_____

whether or not _____

_____

☐ **My student knows the meaning of these words.   Tutor initials _____**

☐ **My student has used the word correctly in a sentence.   Tutor initials _____**   59

Lesson 10 ❖ Power to Change

Scriptures: Matthew 13:3-23, Matthew 8:23-27, Luke 8:22-39, Mark 4:1-41, Mark 5:1-20

Four Kinds of Soil

Wherever Jesus went, large crowds gathered around him, and he used stories to teach them. One day, he told about a farmer who went out to plant his crops, scattering seeds across the field.

Jesus said, "Some seeds fell on a hard path, and birds came and ate them up.

Some seeds fell among rocks, where there was very little soil. The seeds started to grow, but they didn't have strong roots. In the heat of the sun, they withered and died.

Some seeds fell among thorny plants. The seeds started to grow, but were completely choked out.

However, some seeds fell on good soil that had been prepared for planting. There, they grew up to become mature plants. The harvest was great!

Jesus didn't explain the meaning of the parable, so his disciples asked, "What does it mean?"

Jesus answered, "The seed is the Word of God. The different soils show how people receive God's Word. For some, it is like seed that falls on the path. They hear the Word of God, but they don't understand it. Satan comes (like the birds) and takes the seed away, so they will not believe.

For some people, it is like seed that falls among rocks. They gladly receive the Word, but when persecutions come, they have no depth and they give up their faith.

For some people, it is like seed that falls among thorny plants. They receive the Word, but things like worries, money, and pleasures choke out the truth and stop their faith from growing.

Lastly, some people receive the Word like seed that falls on good ground that's been prepared for planting. They hear the Word of God with an open heart, understand it, and their faith grows stronger and stronger!"

Jesus continued to tell the people stories. In fact, he didn't say anything to the crowds without using parables.

Calming a Storm

Jesus taught the crowds all day. In the evening, he said to his disciples, "Let's go to the other side of the lake." So they got into a boat and started across. During the night, a violent storm arose and waves were pushing water into the boat, filling it almost to the point of sinking.

Jesus was in the back of the boat with his head on a cushion, sound asleep. The disciples woke him up, saying, "Master, don't you care that we are going to die?"

Jesus got up and ordered the wind and the waves, "Stop! Be still!" Immediately the wind stopped and the water became calm. Then he turned to his disciples and asked, "Why were you afraid? Don't you have any faith?"

The men were terrified! They asked each other, "Who is this? Even the wind and the sea obey him!"

Healing a Wild Man

Their boat came to shore near a place where a wild man lived among the tombs. People tried to control him, but no one was strong enough. Many times they put him in chains, but he easily broke them off. He wore no clothes. He cried, yelled, and cut himself with stones.

When the wild man saw Jesus and his disciples get out of the boat, he ran and knelt down in front of them. He shouted, "I know who you are! You are Jesus, the Son of the most high God. Leave me alone. Don't torment me."

Jesus ordered the evil spirit, "Come out of the man!" Then he asked, "What is your name?"

The evil spirit answered, "We are called *Legion* because we are many. Please, don't send us into the abyss. Look, there are pigs over on that hill. Send us into them."

Jesus looked at the pigs, and said, "Yes, go there." So, the evil spirits left the man and entered the pigs. All 2,000 of them ran wildly over a cliff, fell into the sea, and were drowned.

The men who were tending the pigs went into the nearby town and told the people what had just happened. A crowd came out to see for themselves. When they got to where Jesus was, they saw the man who had been possessed by evil spirits. He was sitting quietly, fully dressed, and listening to Jesus. The people were filled with fear and asked Jesus to leave their country.

As Jesus and his disciples started to leave, the man who was healed asked to go with them. Jesus told him, "Go back to your people and tell them how much the Lord has done for you."

So the man went back and started telling everyone what Jesus had done for him. All the people who heard him were astonished at how his life was changed!

▢ My student has read the story aloud.   Tutor initials _____

Lesson 10 Review
☐ **Fill in the blanks with the best answer.**

1. Jesus explained the parable to his disciples. "The seed is the _____ of _____, and the different soils show how people _____ God's Word.

2. For some people, it is like seed that falls on the _____. They hear the Word of God, but they don't _____ it. Satan comes and takes the seed away so they will not believe.

3. For some people, it is like seed that falls among _____. They gladly receive the Word, but when _____ come, they have no depth and they give up their faith.

4. For some people it is like seed that falls among _____ plants. They receive the Word, but things like worries, _____, and pleasures choke out the _____ and stop their faith from _____.

5. Lastly, some people receive the Word like seed that falls on _____ ground. They hear the Word of God with an open _____, understand it, and their faith grows stronger and stronger!"

6. One evening, Jesus said to his disciples, "Let's go to the _____ side of the lake."

7. They started across, but during the night, a _____ storm arose. Jesus was in the back of the boat with his head on a cushion, sound _____. The disciples woke him up, saying, "Master, don't you _____ that we are going to _____?"

8. Jesus got up and ordered the wind and the waves, "Stop! Be _____!" Immediately the _____ stopped and the water became calm. Then he turned to his disciples and asked, "Why were you afraid? Don't you have any _____?"

9. The men were _____! They asked each other, "_____ is this? Even the wind and the sea obey him!"

10. Their boat came to shore near where a wild man lived among the _____. People tried to control him, but no one was _____ enough.

11. When the wild man saw Jesus and his disciples get out of the boat, he ran and _____ down in front of them. He shouted, "I _____ who you are! You are Jesus, the _____ of the most high _____. Leave me alone. Don't _____ me!"

12. Jesus _____ the evil spirit, "Come out of the man!" Then he asked, "What is your name?"

13. The evil spirit answered, "We are called *Legion* because we are _____. Please, don't send us into the abyss. Look, there are _____ over on that hill. Send us into them."

14. Jesus said, "_____, go there." So, the evil spirits left the man and entered the pigs. All 2,000 of them _____ wildly over a _____, fell into the sea, and were _____.

15. Soon a crowd of people arrived from the town. When they came to where _____ was, they saw the man who had been _____ by evil spirits. He was sitting _____, fully _____, and listening to Jesus.

16. The people were filled with _____ and asked Jesus to _____ their country.

17. As Jesus and his disciples started to leave, the man who was healed asked to go with them. Jesus said, "Go back to _____ people and tell them how much the _____ has done for you."

☐ **Checked by Tutor**   Tutor initials _____

☐ **My student has told the story aloud in his/her own words.**   Tutor initials _____   61

Reflection and Questions
Lesson 10 ◈ Power to Change

❑ Read the questions on this page.
❑ Tell your thoughts aloud or write your answers on the next page.

Your perspective:

- Tell about a time when someone used a story to teach you a truth.

- What things do people around you worry about?

- Tell about people you know and how they respond to God's Word in different ways.

Search for answers:

- In what ways did Jesus show his power?

Research & Report:

A good example of using a parable to communicate a message is found in II Samuel 11 & 12. King David sinned against God by ordering the murder of a man so he could have his wife. God sent a prophet to confront David. The prophet knew needed to be respectful, and yet it was his responsibility to show the king how awful his sin was. He decided to use a parable. After the prophet told his story, King David understood that he needed to repent and ask God to forgive him.

- Read about this event in *II Samuel 11 & 12*.   ❑ Tell it aloud.

Writing assignment:

- Imagine you are the wild man who used to live among the tombs, but a year ago you were healed. Write several sentences telling how your life has changed over the last year.

Final thoughts:

- What do you think it means to "hear the Word of God with an open heart"?

- Do you feel that God has ever "calmed a storm" in your life? Tell about your experience.

My student's English grammar and sentence structure is correct.   Tutor initials _____

Crossword Puzzle
Use these words.

avoid   community   eat   false   forgive   good   guest

hate   heaven   judged   left   living   loyal   purposely   reputation

Scriptures   soil   sparrow   treat

Across:

2 - If someone does something bad to you, do something ___ for them.

3 - Jews and Samaritans usually tried to ___ each other.

4 - Treat others exactly the way you want them to ___ you.

5 - Peter, James, and John ___ everything and followed Jesus.

7 - If you ___ a person, it is as bad as murder.

9 - Sometimes family members want you to be ___ to them, rather than being loyal to Jesus.

10 - The Holy ___ are the Word of God.

13 - Matthew invited people of low ___ to his home for a meal.

14 - Idols are ___ gods.

16 - Some people thought Jesus should not ___ with sinners.

17 - Jesus offered ___ water to the woman at the well.

Down:

1 - Almost every ___ in Israel had its own synagogue.

2 - When it was time for Mary's baby to be born, there were no ___ rooms available.

6 - Jesus said, "I have the authority to ___ sins.

7 - After his baptism, a voice from ___ spoke words of praise about Jesus.

8 - Jesus ___ traveled through the district of Samaria.

11 - God knows when a ___ falls to the ground.

12 - You will be ___ by the same standards that you judge others.

15 - The parable about four kinds of ___ illustrates how people receive the Word of God.

☐ **Checked by Tutor**   **Tutor initials** _____

Certificate of Achievement

_____

has completed all the lessons in

Language Olympics

Advanced Studies - Book 1

Congratulations!

Tutor Signature _____

Date _____

Our Mission

Sharing the story of God for discipleship using all the stories of the Bible.

Our Websites

BibleTelling.org – all BibleTelling news, events, and services (including Seminars in Israel, Training, and free download of All the Stories of the Bible)

BTStories.com – free online access to audio, video, text, timeline, map, and insights for *All the Stories of the Bible*

ChristianStorytelling.com – official website of the annual conference

LanguageOlympics.org – literacy and ESL training using 60 Bible stories

Our Media and Resources

YouTube video series: https://bit.ly/2rLOZFY – The Art of Storytelling

Creative Communication Skills video playlist – Wistia http://wi.st/2tEQRSF

Amazon books/ebooks: https://amzn.to/2j7LER2 – Author page for John Walsh

Amazon books/ebooks: https://amzn.to/2Tpzcup – Author page for Jan Walsh

Story of the Day Subscription

Receive an e-mail each weekday with links to the video, audio, and narrative of the story of the day.

E-mail your subscription request to **info@BibleTelling.com**.

Facebook

Search for "BibleTelling"

Mobile App

Search for "BT Stories" in the Apple, Android, and Windows app stores

Contact

E-mail us at info@BibleTelling.com with any questions.

Post comments or questions on our Facebook page.

BibleTelling
2905 Gill Street
Bloomington, IL 61704

Made in the USA
Middletown, DE
22 May 2022

66065677R00038